A TEEN GUIDE to Quick, Healthy SNACKS

by Dana Meachen Rau

CONTENT ADVISER: Joan Bushman, RD, MPH, Dietician and Wellness Specialist

READING ADVISER: Alexa L. Sandmann, EdD, Professor of Literacy, College and Graduate School of Education, Health, and Human Services, Kent State University

COMPASS POINT BOOKS
a capstone imprint

Compass Point Books
151 Good Counsel Drive
P.O. Box 669
Mankato, MN 56002-0669

Editor: Jennifer Fretland VanVoorst
Designers: Veronica Correia and Heidi Thompson
Media Researcher: Wanda Winch
Food Stylist: Sarah Schuette
Library Consultant: Kathleen Baxter
Production Specialist: Sarah Bennett

Image Credits

ArtParts Stock Illustrations, illustrations of food and kitchen objects throughout book; Capstone Studio: Karon Dubke, cover (top all), 15, 17, 19, 21, 23, 24 (all), 27, 29, 31, 33, 37, 39, 41, 43, 45, 49, 51, 53; Dana Meachen Rau, 64 (middle), iStockphoto: Cat London, 62, digitalskillet, 25, Evgeniy Gorbunov, 57, iodrakon, 34–35, nullplus, 59 (left); Shutterstock: Andrejs Pidjass, 60, Andrjuss, back cover, Ann Worthy, 8, archana bhartia, 1, AVAVA, 59 (right), D McKenzie, 12, Dmitry Baevskiy, 7, Drozdowski, 6–7 (bottom), Elena Schweitzer, 54 (top), Elke Dennis, cover (bottom middle left), 5, George Do gikh, cover (bottom middle right), Ian O'Hanlon, 100% stamp used throughout book, Julia Petukhova, 47, Kameel4u, 9, Kati Molin, cover (bottom right), 13 (top), kiboka, 46, Lana Langlois, 13 (bottom), Maksim Shmeljov, 58–59 (bottom), 62–63 (bottom), 64 (bottom), Mehmet Dilsiz, cover (bottom left), Monkey Business Images, 63, Natalia Siverina, 47 (popcorn), Olga Lyubkina, cover background, Thaiview, 10–11 (background).

Library of Congress Cataloging-in-Publication Data
Rau, Dana Meachen, 1971–
  A Teen guide to quick, healthy snacks / by Dana Meachen Rau.
    p. cm. — (Teen cookbooks)
    title: Quick, healthy snacks
  Includes index.
  Summary: "Information and recipes help readers create quick,
healthy, and tasty snacks"—Provided by publisher.
    ISBN 978-0-7565-4406-5 (library binding)
  1. Snack foods—Juvenile literature. 2. Cookbooks. I. Title. II. Title:
Quick, healthy snacks.
  TX740.R39 2011
    641.5'3—dc22   2010040681

Visit Compass Point Books on the Internet at *www.capstonepub.com*

Printed in the United States of America in North Mankato, Minnesota.

092010   005933CGS11

TABLE OF CONTENTS

TEAM SWEET OR TEAM SALTY?

You know the feeling. It starts in the pit of your stomach. The grumbling. The rumbling. The growling. At first you're the only one who can hear it. But it grows.

Soon you imagine food everywhere. Your eraser suddenly resembles a stick of gum. Your friend's curly hair couldn't really be a bowl of spaghetti, could it? As you chew on your pencil, you can't help wishing it were really a candy bar.

Now your friends can hear the growling. Your stomach is like a wild animal. It can't be tamed. It's hungry. You have to feed it. Time for a snack.

Snacks are like minimeals. They take the edge off your hunger to tide you over until the next meal. Some people can make it from breakfast to lunch to dinner with no snacks in between. Other people like to graze their way through the day.

So what do you like to snack on? Do you get excited about chocolate bars, apples, and cookies? If you answered yes, then you're on Team Sweet. Or would you be happier with pretzels, peanuts, or crackers? Congratulations! You've been picked for Team Salty. Perhaps you have trouble taking sides. If you satisfy your snack cravings with chocolate dipped pretzels, then you are a fan of both—sweet and salty.

You might find you're hungriest when you come home after school. (For some reason, school seems to suck all of the energy right out of you!) But before you start raiding the refrigerator, clearing out the cupboard, or pilfering the pantry, think about what you're grabbing to eat. Whether you're on Team Sweet or Team Salty, not all snacks are good for your body. Find the ones that give your body the fuel it needs, and then chow down. Tame the growling beast with a healthful snack.

Down almost every aisle of the grocery store, you may be tempted by packaged snacks. A bag of mini cookies. A container of chips. Crackers and cheese sauce that come with a handy spreader.

Don't let the food companies tell you how to snack! You can prepare your own snacks with fresher ingredients. Not only will they be healthier for you, but they'll use less packaging, and that's better for the environment.

Produce

Fruits are one of the best ready-to-eat foods. Just peel a banana or an orange and you have the perfect snack inside. But sometimes it's hard to tell from the outside whether a fruit is fresh. Most fruits are firm when unripe and soften as they ripen. If they have brown or soft spots, they are either rotten or on their way. Look for vegetables that are brightly colored and firm, not limp, soft, or discolored.

The best way to get fresh produce is to buy fruits and veggies that are in season where you live. Grocery stores sometimes buy from local farms. You may be able to visit a pick-your-own farm or buy your produce at a farmers market. Then you'll know it's fresh.

Refrigerated Foods

Refrigerated foods need to be kept cold so they don't spoil. But even in the fridge, they will spoil after a while. That's why these foods are marked with "use by" dates. After that date the food is no longer safe to eat. So look for these dates on meats, poultry, fish, dairy foods, and eggs. Don't buy it if the date has passed.

Organics

You may notice the word "organic" stamped on everything from lettuce to yogurt. A food can be completely organic, or it may have organic ingredients. Organic farmers use natural ways to feed, protect, and weed their crops and raise their livestock. Because they are not grown with artifical chemicals, organic foods are often more healthy for you and for the environment.

Packaged Foods

You can't avoid packaged foods altogether. But be smart about the ones you buy. Pasta, crackers, cereal, and anything else in a box, bag, or can have nutrition labels. Here's where you can read about how healthful a food is. The nutrition label lists how much fat, sugar, protein, carbohydrates, and sodium an item contains. It also tells you the serving size. While many packaged foods do not spoil, the "best if used by" date will let you know when the item is best to eat.

HOW TO AVOID ...

... Upsetting The Grownups.

Do your parents accuse you of being a tornado when you come home from school, tossing your backpack on the floor, kicking your shoes into the corner, and spreading your homework all over the kitchen table? Try not to be so messy while you prepare your snack.

You can slip on a spill if you don't mop it up or cut yourself on a knife that you leave out by mistake. When you're done in the kitchen, put foods back in the refrigerator so they don't spoil. Close the box of crackers so it doesn't go stale. Wash the dishes and wipe down the counters. Make sure you've turned off the stove if you used it. Cleaning up will score major points with the adults in your house.

... Burning The House Down.

A fire can start with just a tiny spark, so keep a fire extinguisher in the kitchen. The flame from a gas stove can spread especially easily. Be smart when using the stove. Never place something flammable close to a burner. Keep loose clothing, oven mitts, and kitchen towels away from the stove so they don't ignite.

... A Trip To The Emergency Room.

Did you know sharp knives are actually safer than dull ones? Dull knives can slip off of food and cut into your finger instead. But you need to pay very close attention when you use a sharp knife. Watch while you cut, and immediately clean the knife and put it away when you are done.

Be careful of hot pots on the stove. Avoid knocking them over by pointing handles to the back of the stove instead of letting them hang over the edge. Prevent steam from billowing into your face when you open a hot pot by lifting the lid away from you. Always wear oven mitts when taking something out of the oven or the microwave.

Electricity and water don't mix, so don't use a plug-in appliance too close to the sink or a puddle of water. Never put your hand into an appliance that's plugged in, such as a toaster or blender. And don't stretch the cord over an open area where someone could trip and knock the appliance off the counter.

... Seeing Your Snack Come Back Again.

If you use spoiled, expired, or unclean food for making your snacks, you run the risk of getting sick and seeing that snack come back again.

To eliminate the bacteria that can make you sick, wash your hands with hot, soapy water before any session in the kitchen. Fruits and vegetables may look clean, but you don't know where they've been on their trip to the grocery store. Gently rub fruits and vegetables under cool running water.

High temperatures kill bacteria. That's why you need to cook some foods completely before you eat them. And even though you're tempted to taste the batter if you're making brownies, you don't want to eat uncooked eggs.

Low temperatures slow the growth of bacteria. That's why all meats, eggs, and dairy foods, and most fruits and veggies need to stay in the refrigerator. After a while, they'll spoil even in

there. If the milk smells sour, an apple feels mushy, or the bread has mold, don't risk it. Throw it away.

After you cook, wash all of your kitchen gear in the dishwasher or in the sink with very hot water. If germs are left to hang out there, you could pick them up the next time you cook.

The kitchen is your domain! Wipe out those germs before they take over.

HOW TO USE THIS BOOK

The recipes in this book are designed to be quick and easy. After all, when you're hungry for a snack, you need it *now!* Every recipe is divided into three sections. The list of ingredients is called Food Stuff. All the tools you'll need are called Kitchen Gear. The Prep Steps are the step-by-step instructions for making your snacks.

If you don't know the difference between a saucepan and a stockpot or how mashing differs from mincing, check the Tools Glossary (page 56) and the Technique Glossary (page 58). These glossaries will help you learn about unfamiliar kitchen terms.

These recipes are flexible. Increase or decrease the amount of ingredients of a recipe depending on how many people are noshing with you. If you have the whole gymnastics team over after school, make more of a recipe. If it's just you and your cat lounging in a sunny spot, make enough for one.

If you're a vegetarian, you're in luck. All of the recipes in this book are meatless.

Conversion Charts

WEIGHT

UNITED STATES	METRIC
1 ounce	30 grams
½ pound	225 g
1 pound	455 g

TEMPERATURE

DEGREES FAHRENHEIT	DEGREES CELSIUS
250°F	120°C
300°F	150°C
350°F	180°C
375°F	190°C
400°F	200°C
425°F	220°C

Look for special stamps on some recipes:

If you have a sweet tooth, look for the **Team Sweet** stamp. If you're more of a salty dog, look for **Team Salty**.

Team Sweet

Team Salty

Picky eater? Some of the recipes can be adapted to fit your tastes. Check out the *Call in the Subs* stamp for alternatives to some of the ingredients in the Food Stuff lists.

	UNITED STATES	METRIC
VOLUME	¼ teaspoon	1 milliliter
	½ teaspoon	2.5 mL
	1 teaspoon	5 mL
	1 tablespoon	15 mL
	¼ cup	60 mL
	⅓ cup	80 mL
	½ cup	120 mL
	1 cup	250 mL
	1 quart	1 liter

GET READY TO TAME THAT GROWLING STOMACH WITH A QUICK STOP IN THE KITCHEN.

SWEET SWEETS

It's the weekend. Sweet. And you've got a sweet day planned! You don't want to run out of steam in the middle of your adventures, so be sure to grab a snack. Brownies, cookies, nuts, and fruit are all treats you can take with you for a quick burst of energy in the middle of your day. Go Team Sweet!

ARE YOU KIDDING ME? ZUCCHINI BROWNIES

Some secrets will never be uncovered. Who carved the huge heads on Easter Island? Does Bigfoot really exist? Why do clothes dryers always eat your socks? It's up to you to decide whether you want to reveal the secret of these moist and delicious brownies. But even if you told, would anyone believe you? They'll fall over, gasping, "Zucchini? Are you kidding me?"

Food Stuff

¼ cup cocoa powder

1 cup whole wheat flour

½ teaspoon baking soda

¼ teaspoon baking powder

⅛ teaspoon salt

½ cup white sugar

¼ cup applesauce

¼ cup plain yogurt

1 cup grated zucchini

1 large egg, lightly beaten

½ cup chocolate chunks

Vegetable cooking spray

Kitchen Gear

Medium and large mixing bowls

Dry measuring cups

Measuring spoons

Spatula

8- x 8-inch (20- x 20-centimeter) baking pan

Knife

Makes 16 brownies

Prep Steps

1. Preheat the oven to 350°F.

2. In a medium-sized bowl, mix the cocoa powder, flour, baking soda, baking powder, and salt with a spatula.

3. In a large bowl, mix the sugar, applesauce, yogurt, zucchini, and egg.

4. Pour the dry mixture into the wet mixture. Stir with a spatula until well combined. Stir in the chocolate chunks.

5. Spray an 8- x 8-inch (20- x 20-cm) pan with cooking spray.

6. Pour the batter into the pan, spreading evenly with the spatula.

7. Bake at 350°F for 20 to 25 minutes or until a toothpick inserted in the center comes out clean.

8. Let the pan cool. Cut the brownies into squares with a sharp knife.

Tips for Measuring Flour

Flour needs to be light and airy to get an accurate measurement. If you need a cup of flour, don't dip the whole measuring cup into your flour bag. The flour will be too tightly packed inside. Instead, spoon the flour into the cup a little at a time. Level off the top with the straight side of a table knife so it is completely flat and level with the brim. Then you'll have the right amount.

The Toothpick Test

Bakers test to see whether food is done by inserting a toothpick in the center of brownies (or cake, muffins, etc.) and pulling it out again. If gooey batter is clinging to the toothpick, the food needs to bake longer. But if the toothpick comes out clean, your treat is done, and you can chow down.

SUPER SMART COOKIES

This cookie doesn't know the speed of light or the meaning of $E=mc^2$. It doesn't know how to knit a sweater or build a tree house. But it is smart. It's made with ingredients that are much more healthful than those in store-bought cookies. When you make cookies yourself, you know what goes into them. When you eat them, you know what's going into you. That's not just smart. That's super smart.

Food Stuff

1 cup whole wheat flour

1 cup unbleached all-purpose flour

1 teaspoon baking powder

¼ teaspoon baking soda

4 ounces soft tofu

¼ cup vegetable oil

¼ cup applesauce

1 teaspoon vanilla

¼ cup white sugar

¾ cup packed brown sugar

½ cup semisweet chocolate chips

Vegetable cooking spray

Kitchen Gear

Medium and large mixing bowls

Dry measuring cups

Liquid measuring cup

Measuring spoons

Blender

Electric hand mixer

Spatula

Turner

Tablespoon

Baking sheet

Wire cooling rack

Makes two dozen cookies

Prep Steps

1. Preheat oven to 375°F.

2. In a medium bowl, mix together the flours, baking powder, and baking soda. Set aside.

3. In a blender, puree the tofu until it is smooth. Pour the tofu into in a large bowl. Add the oil, applesauce, vanilla, and sugars. Beat these together with an electric hand mixer until well combined.

4. Add the flour mixture to the wet mixture. Beat together.

5. Add the chocolate chips, and stir with a spatula.

6. Spray the baking sheet with vegetable cooking spray.

7. Scoop out rounded tablespoons of dough. Roll into balls to form the cookies. Place them onto the baking sheet about two inches (5 cm) apart.

8. Bake at 375°F for 10 to 12 minutes or until browned.

9. Let the cookies sit for at least two minutes. Then transfer with a turner to a wire cooling rack.

Tofu Who?

Tofu is made from soybeans and packed with nutrients. It has lots of protein and calcium but very little fat. Adding tofu to a cookie recipe means you don't have to use an egg, which is good news if you are allergic to eggs or if you want to go vegan. A vegan doesn't eat any products from animals—not just meat, but eggs and dairy products too.

Call in the Subs

If you're not a chocolate fan, replace the chocolate chips with chips of another flavor, such as butterscotch or white chocolate, or with raisins or dried fruit. You can also add ½ cup of chopped walnuts.

MIX IT UP

It's hard to decide where to look at a three-ring circus. Should you watch the flame swallower balanced on the ball or the motorcycles zipping around in the spherical cage? And how many clowns just came out of the trunk of that tiny car?

With fruit, chocolate, and nuts, this snack is like a three-ring circus in a bowl. And the best part is that in a bowl, you can enjoy all the rings at once.

Food Stuff

½ cup whole almonds

½ cup dried cherries

⅓ cup semisweet chocolate chunks

Kitchen Gear

Dry measuring cups

Bowl

Makes two servings

Prep Steps

1. Mix together all the ingredients in a bowl. That's it!

Big Batch

You can double, triple, or even quadruple the quantities in this recipe to make a large batch. Keep it in an airtight container so you can easily reach in for a handful in a hurry.

Team Sweet

Team Salty

Call in the Subs

Peanuts, pecans, and walnuts also taste good mixed with fruit and chocolate.

POMEGRANATE APPLE SLOP

Do you hate going to the doctor? The crinkly paper on the examination table, the cold stethoscope on your back, and no matter how old you get, no one likes shots. Some people say, "An apple a day keeps the doctor away." But many studies show that pomegranates are great for your health too. They contain nutrients that keep your blood flowing and help lower bad cholesterol.

Maybe if you eat enough of this applesauce with a kick of pomegranate, you'll be able to avoid the doctor for a while!

Team Sweet

Food Stuff

3 pounds of apples (about 6 or 7 apples)

¾ cup pomegranate juice

2 tablespoons lemon juice

2 tablespoons packed brown sugar

1 teaspoon cinnamon

Kitchen Gear

Vegetable peeler

Knife

6-quart stockpot

Spoon

Potato masher

Makes about 10 ½-cup servings

Prep Steps

1. Peel the skin off the apples with a vegetable peeler. Cut each apple in half, cut out the core, and slice each half into about four pieces.

2. Combine apples, pomegranate juice, lemon juice, sugar, and cinnamon in the stockpot. Stir together with a spoon.

3. Cook over high heat until the liquid starts to boil. Then turn heat to low and cook for about 15 to 20 minutes or until the apples are very soft.

4. Take the pot off the heat. Mash the apples with a potato masher until no large chunks remain.

Warm Apple Pie

This applesauce tastes like apple pie, but without the crust. If you don't have the chance to eat it right away and you want it warm, heat it in the microwave for about 30 seconds. As with apple pie, you can also have it á la mode. (That means with a little ice cream on the top!)

Hold The Sugar

Some apples are sweeter than others, so you may not need as much sugar as the recipe calls for. If you use a tart apple, like a Granny Smith, use the full amount of sugar given in the recipe. But if you use a sweeter apple, use less. When the applesauce is done, have a taste. If it needs more sugar, you can add it then.

QUICK PEACH AND BLACKBERRY CRISP

Some grandmas spend hours in their warm, cozy kitchens slicing fresh peaches, sifting flour, and grating cinnamon sticks to make you a perfect fruit crisp. But sometimes you may want the taste when Grandma's not around. So make it yourself. It's just as good, and a lot faster too.

Food Stuff

⅓ cup granola (with or without raisins)

1 teaspoon packed brown sugar

1 tablespoon chopped pecans

1 cup sliced peaches (fresh or canned)

½ cup fresh blackberries

Kitchen Gear

Dry measuring cups

Measuring spoons

Bowl

Spoon

Colander

Microwave

Makes one serving

Prep Steps

1. In a small microwave-safe bowl, mix the granola, brown sugar, and pecans with a spoon.

2. Drain the peaches in a colander. Add them to the bowl with the granola mixture.

3. Rinse the blackberries with cold water and pat dry. Add them to the bowl.

4. Mix the fruit and granola together.

5. Microwave uncovered on high for one minute. Take out the bowl and stir. Cook for another 30 seconds if it isn't warm enough yet.

Too Sweet

Canned fruit can have a lot of added sugar. Look for canned fruits packed in their own juices or in water. Avoid canned fruit packed in heavy syrup. And use fresh fruits if possible to avoid extra sugar and for best taste.

23

AFTER SCHOOL PROTEIN PUNCH

Do you come home from school with a voracious appetite? Before you start gnawing on the table, take a moment to make a protein snack to fill you up. Protein will help tame your appetite till dinnertime. And your parents will appreciate a table without teeth marks.

SPICY NUTS

Squirrels love nuts, so keep those wild animals away from this snack. If they try these spicy nuts, they'll never want to go back to plain old nuts. Eat them up before you find them buried all over your yard.

Food Stuff

2 cups unsalted peanuts

1 tablespoon butter

1 tablespoon lime juice

2 teaspoons sugar

½ teaspoon salt

1 teaspoon chili powder

Kitchen Gear

Dry measuring cups

Measuring spoons

Microwave

Bowl

Spoon

Large baking pan

Makes 2 cups

Prep Steps

1. Preheat the oven to 300°F.

2. Place the butter in a microwave-safe bowl. Heat it in the microwave on high for 30 seconds to a minute, until it melts.

3. Take the bowl out of the microwave. Add the peanuts and the lime juice. Stir well until the peanuts are coated in the butter.

4. Pour the peanuts into a single layer in the baking pan.

5. Bake the peanuts for about 35 minutes at 300°F or until toasted. Stir a few times during baking.

6. Take the pan out of the oven. While the peanuts are still warm, sprinkle with the sugar, salt, and chili powder. Stir well. Eat warm or cool.

Team Sweet

Team Salty

Call in the Subs

If you're allergic to peanuts, you can still enjoy this snack. Just try another nut. Almonds, cashews, and pecans taste great with a little sweet and salty spice too. But check with a parent or guardian before you try any substitutions in case peanuts aren't your only allergy.

THOSE LITTLE DEVILS

Is that deviled egg looking at you? Is he a nice egg? Or a little devil? Maybe he thinks you're cute. Maybe he wants to copy your social studies homework. Maybe he just wants to be your snack.

You won't know until you try him.

Food Stuff

6 large eggs

3 tablespoons nonfat plain yogurt

¾ teaspoon spicy brown mustard

Salt and pepper

Black olives, sliced

Green onions, sliced lengthwise

Kitchen Gear

2-quart saucepan

Measuring spoons

Knife

Spoon

Small mixing bowl

Plate

Fork

Makes a dozen egg halves

Prep Steps

1. Place the eggs in the saucepan. Add just enough cold water to cover the eggs.

2. Cover and heat on high until the water boils. Turn off the heat and let sit for 15 minutes.

3. Drain the hot water off the eggs into the sink. Add cold water to the pan. Let the pan sit for a moment. Then drain off the water and fill with cold water again. This cools the eggs gradually.

4. When the eggs are cool enough to handle, peel off the shells.

5. Cut each egg in half lengthwise. Scoop the yolk into a bowl. Set aside the whites on a plate.

6. Add the yogurt and mustard to the bowl. Mix with a fork until creamy. Add salt and pepper to taste.

7. Spoon the yolk mixture back into the holes in the eggs.

8. Decorate with slices of olives and green onions.

Make It a Party

To make enough eggs for party appetizers, increase the number of eggs to a dozen; use 5 tablespoons of yogurt and 1½ teaspoons of mustard. With each egg cut in half, you'll have two dozen half eggs in all.

What Are You Looking AT?

If you don't like a snack that looks back at you, use this recipe to make egg salad instead. Chop the hard boiled eggs (the whites and the yolks) into small pieces, and mix with the rest of the ingredients in the recipe. Serve it on toast or over lettuce.

TOP 10 HUMMUS

Don't judge hummus by its pasty texture or plain color. Hummus is a taste sensation to jazz up any afternoon. And with at least 10 ways to prepare it, you'll have trouble deciding how to rank your favorites.

Food Stuff

1 16-ounce can garbanzo beans (chickpeas)
2 tablespoons olive oil
2 tablespoons plain nonfat yogurt
1 tablespoon lemon juice
½ teaspoon cumin
½ teaspoon salt
¼ teaspoon garlic powder
Pita chips
Cucumber, sliced

Kitchen Gear

Colander
Liquid measuring cup
Measuring spoons
Mixing bowl
Hand blender

Makes 1 cup hummus

Prep Steps

1. Open the can of garbanzo beans and drain in a colander.

2. Combine the first seven ingredients in a bowl (garbanzo beans through garlic powder). Blend with a hand blender until smooth.

3. Spread on pita chips or sliced cucumbers.

4. If you want to add a little extra flavor to this basic hummus, here are 10 possible things to stir in after you have blended the hummus:

   Roasted garlic
   Kalamata olives, sliced
   Jalapeño peppers, minced
   Roasted red peppers, minced
   Dried basil and sun-dried tomatoes, minced
   Pine nuts, toasted
   Ground black pepper
   Crumbled feta cheese
   Roasted eggplant, diced
   Green onions, sliced

Spread The Goodness Around

Hummus is a tasty spread on crackers. But it's also a good dip for vegetables at a party. Spread it on sandwiches too.

POKE-IT-IN PEANUT BUTTER POPS

Peanut butter makes friends easily—probably because he's so sticky. Other foods just can't seem to keep away from his magnetic personality. You may like to eat peanut butter right out of the jar with a spoon. But take a few minutes to jazz up that spoonful with some healthful decorations.

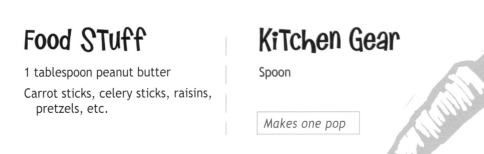

Food Stuff

1 tablespoon peanut butter

Carrot sticks, celery sticks, raisins, pretzels, etc.

Kitchen Gear

Spoon

Makes one pop

Prep Steps

1. Fill a spoon with about a tablespoon of peanut butter.

2. Poke in carrots, celery, raisins, pretzels, bananas, berries, apples, cereal or anything else that you think goes well with peanut butter.

3. Eat it like a lollipop.

Team Sweet

Team Salty

Call in the Subs

There are other butters besides peanut butter. Nuts or seeds are ground to make almond butter, cashew butter, and sunflower seed butter too.

VEG OUT WITH VEGGIES

Have you refined hanging out to an art form? Do you like resting in the recliner? Lounging on the lawn chair? Chilling on the couch? You need a snack to go with all that relaxing. Veg out with veggies!

FRESH SALSA

Salsa has an attitude—she's fresh. She snubs other dips. She turns up her nose at stale chips. She makes fun of mild cheese.

But that doesn't mean salsa has bad manners. When salsa's made from fresh veggies, fresh is good. It's not rude—it's delicious.

Food STuff

2 cups diced tomatoes

¼ cup diced red onion

½ cup chopped black olives

1 4.5-ounce can chopped green chilies

½ cup frozen corn, thawed

1 tablespoon white vinegar

2 teaspoons garlic powder

Salt and pepper

KiTchen Gear

Knife

Mixing bowl

Liquid measuring cup

Dry measuring cups

Measuring spoons

Spoon

Makes 4 cups

Prep STeps

1. Place the diced tomato, onion, and olives in a mixing bowl.

2. Add the chilies and corn. Mix together.

3. Add the vinegar and garlic powder. Add salt and pepper to taste. Stir well.

4. Store in an airtight container in the refrigerator until you are ready to use it. The longer it sits, the stronger the flavor.

Team Salty

Call in the Subs

Salsa comes in many varieties. You can also add in ½ cup of diced avocado, mango, or peaches. If you like the taste of lime, replace the 1 tablespoon of vinegar with 1 tablespoon of lime juice.

ROCKIN' GUACAMOLE

It's not easy being green. For years guacamole has been battling with salsa for the title of "best dip for chips." So make them both. Then decide which one gets to be on top—of your nachos.

Food Stuff

1 ripe avocado

½ cup diced tomatoes

1 tablespoon diced red onion

½ teaspoon chili powder

½ teaspoon lime juice

Salt and pepper

Makes about 1 cup

Kitchen Gear

Dry measuring cups

Measuring spoons

Knife

Spoon

Bowl

Fork

Team Salty

Prep Steps

1. Slice the avocado in half. Take out the pit and scoop the flesh into a bowl with a spoon.

2. With the back of a fork, mash the avocado until no lumps remain.

3. Add the diced tomatoes and onion to the avocado. Add the chili powder and lime juice. Sprinkle in salt and pepper to taste. Mix together.

4. Serve immediately.

Quick Nachos

Now that you've made the dips (the salsa and the guacamole), you need to eat them with chips! Make a quick batch of nachos. On a microwave-safe plate, lay out some tortilla chips. Sprinkle on some grated cheddar cheese. Microwave uncovered on high for about 20 to 30 seconds, or until the cheese melts. Remove from the microwave and top with sliced black olives, sliced jalapeños, and black beans. Top the chips with salsa, guacamole, or both.

Avocado Cutting Tips

Slice the avocado down the center lengthwise. When you open it, there will be a round pit in the middle. To remove the pit, run the knife along the edge of the pit. Then use your fingers to loosen it and pop it out.

SALTY EDAMAME

Ed was a fun dog. He knew lots of tricks. One day Ed had puppies, and we found out Ed wasn't a boy dog—Ed a mommy! Use that bad joke to remember the name of these tasty soybeans.

Food Stuff

2 cups water
Frozen edamame in pods (about 50 pods)
Salt

Makes one ½-cup serving

Kitchen Gear

2-quart saucepan
Liquid measuring cup
Colander
Bowl

Prep Steps

1. Fill the saucepan with 2 cups of cold water. Place on the stovetop and heat covered on high until the water boils.

2. Add the edamame pods to the water. Return to a boil, then set the timer and cook uncovered for about five minutes.

3. Drain the edamame in a colander and rinse with cold water. Place the pods in a bowl.

4. Sprinkle salt over the edamame pods.

5. Eat the edamame by squeezing the pods. Open your mouth and pop the soybeans right in. Don't eat the pods. You can place them in a separate bowl, then throw them away or put them in the compost when you're done.

Team Salty

Stop That Shaker

Remember: Too much salt = bad. By salting the edamame when they are still in the pods, you get the taste of the salt on your fingers as you eat them. But you consume less salt than if you shucked all the edamame and then sprinkled salt on the beans.

OLIVE YOU SPREAD

It's more than just a crush. It's an infatuation. It's an obsession. No one in the world has ever loved a food as much as you'll love this one. You'll be shouting over the school loudspeaker: "Olive You Spread!"

Food Stuff

1 tablespoon olive oil

½ cup black pitted olives

½ cup Spanish manzanilla olives stuffed with pimientos

⅛ teaspoon black pepper

¼ teaspoon ground dried thyme

1 tablespoon chopped walnuts

Crackers

Kitchen Gear

Blender

Liquid measuring cup

Dry measuring cups

Measuring spoons

Makes about ½ cup

Prep Steps

1. Combine all of the above ingredients in a blender. Blend them until they form a paste.

2. Spread on crackers.

Team Salty

Spruce up a Sandwich

You can use this spread on sandwiches too. If you're in the mood for a hearty snack, try Olive You Spread on crusty Italian bread with salami, pepperoni, provolone cheese, and a slice of tomato.

HIGH KICK TOMATO JUICE

It's safe to say you should avoid getting kicked in the mouth during a game, match, or, well, pretty much anytime. But it's OK to get a kick in the mouth from this juice. Its hot combination of vegetable flavors will have you seeing stars.

Food Stuff

1 cup tomato juice

¼ cup carrot juice

1 teaspoon lemon juice

1 teaspoon horseradish

¼ teaspoon hot pepper sauce

Fresh ground pepper

Kitchen Gear

Liquid measuring cup

Measuring spoons

Drinking glass

Spoon

Makes one 10-ounce serving

Prep Steps

1. Pour the tomato juice into a glass. Add the carrot and lemon juices.

2. Spoon in the horseradish and hot sauce. Stir well with a spoon.

3. Top with fresh ground pepper to taste.

GLUTTON FOR GRAINS

When you need a burst of energy, surround yourself with acres of amber waves of grain. From wheat to corn to rice and more, the carbohydrates in grains will give you the energy to keep you going well past sundown.

QUICK MAC

Even foods have friends. Cookies and milk, salt and pepper, peanut butter and jelly, franks and beans, ketchup and mustard ...

But mac and cheese? They're more than just friends. They're BFFs.

Food Stuff

½ cup whole wheat elbow macaroni (dry)
¼ cup part-skim ricotta cheese
½ teaspoon dried parsley
¼ teaspoon dried basil
⅛ teaspoon red pepper flakes
Salt and pepper

Kitchen Gear

2-quart saucepan
Dry measuring cups
Measuring spoons
Spoon
Bowl

Makes one serving

Team Salty

Prep Steps

1. Fill the saucepan with about 1 quart of water. Heat on high on the stove until it comes to a boil. Add the macaroni and cook uncovered according to the package directions, about eight to 10 minutes.

2. Drain the macaroni in the sink in a colander. Return the macaroni to the warm pan.

3. Add the ricotta, parsley, basil, and red pepper flakes. Stir well.

4. Serve in a bowl. Add salt and pepper to taste.

PARM AND PEPPER POPCORN

Why are people in the movies so dense? Do those characters really think camping out next to the swamp monster's hideout is a good idea? No matter how dumb they are, you can't wait for the scene when the slimy arm reaches into their tent. Make this popcorn before the movie starts so you don't miss a moment.

Team Salty

Food Stuff

1 bag microwave popcorn, light butter flavor

¼ cup dry Parmesan cheese

Ground black pepper

Vegetable cooking spray

Kitchen Gear

Microwave

Bowl

Dry measuring cups

Spoon

Makes about 7 cups—about two servings

Prep Steps

1. Pop the bag of popcorn in the microwave according to the directions on the package.

2. Pour about a third of the popped corn into a large bowl. Spray it with vegetable cooking spray, gently stirring as you spray to get all the pieces covered.

3. Sprinkle about one third of the cheese, and some pepper, onto the popcorn.

4. Pour in another third of the popcorn, spray with oil, and sprinkle with a third of the cheese and more pepper.

5. Pour in the rest of the popcorn, spray with oil, and top with the remaining cheese and some more pepper.

6. Stir well until the popcorn is well coated and there is no more dry cheese at the bottom of the bowl.

Spray Oil vs. Butter

Vegetable cooking spray is oil in an aerosol container. It keeps food from sticking to pans when you cook. It can also replace butter for popcorn. You need some sort of oil to help the cheese stick to the popcorn. With cooking spray, you consume a smaller amount of fat than if you dosed your popcorn with melted butter.

TOP IT OFF

Sometimes you have a perfect day. An A on your science experiment. An unexpected present from your parents. A canceled history quiz. What would top off such an amazing chain of events? A rice cake topped with a perfect combination of sweet and salty.

Food Stuff

1 unsalted rice cake

3 thin slices of apple

1 ounce sharp cheddar cheese

Kitchen Gear

Knife

Makes one serving

Prep Steps

1. Cut the cheddar cheese into one or more thin slices. Place on top of the rice cake.

2. Lay the apple slices on top of the cheese.

A Great Base

Rice cakes make a great base for anything you ordinarily eat or spread on bread or crackers. Try a rice cake with guacamole (page 38), hummus (page 30), or anything else you can think of!

Team Sweet

Team Salty

53

CHEW ON THIS!

Snacks are supposed to be quick and easy. They're not supposed to be meals. It is quick to run to a snack bar for a small order of fries. It is easy to open the cabinet and grab a bag of cookies. But choose the wrong kind of snack and you might be consuming a whole meal's worth of calories.

When you reach for a bag of chips or a can of soda, do your parents whine that you eat too much junk food? Adults can be so negative. Think positive instead. Learn about what's good for you, and make positive decisions about your snacks. Your body will thank you.

CARBOHYDRATES

There's a reason lots of people are on Team Sweet. Your body needs sugar. Carbohydrates are sugars that your body turns into energy. Grains, fruits, and vegetables contain carbohydrates.

Grains: Some of the most common grains are wheat, rice, oats, and corn. Crackers,

breads, and pasta are all made from grain. It's best to eat whole grain foods, not foods made with refined grains. Whole grains still contain their vital nutrients. Refined grains are stripped of the good stuff.

Fruits and vegetables: Fruits and vegetables have valuable vitamins and minerals. Some are easily snackable—an apple can fit right in your backpack. Veggies are great in dips for a quick bite between meals.

But a food isn't good for you just because it contains sugar. Your body turns sugary soda and candy into energy too. But those foods have no other nutrients. They fill you up so you don't have room for more healthful foods. And they can rot your teeth.

PROTEIN

Protein is a vital part of your diet— you can't have healthy bones or muscles without it. You probably get most of your protein at mealtimes if you eat meat, poultry, and fish. But snacks can be a good source of protein too.

Eggs: Since eggs are so quick to cook, you can whip up a snack in a jiffy.

Beans: Beans are bite-sized bits of protein that you can easily pop in your mouth.

Nuts: A handful of mixed nuts is an easy snack to nibble when you need a quick bite. Or spread peanut butter on some crackers for a tasty crunch.

Dairy products: Dairy snacks, such as a cup of yogurt or a slice of cheese, also contain calcium, which helps strengthen your bones.

FAT

Your body needs fat to store energy—but that doesn't mean you should start drizzling melted butter over your popcorn. You don't need to seek out sources of fat, because many foods have fat in them already. You do need to avoid extra fats. Try to buy low fat or nonfat dairy foods. Don't spread too much butter on your roll. Keep away from fried foods, which have been cooked in fat.

It is better to get fats from nuts, plant oils such as olive oil and vegetable oil, and foods such as olives and avocados, than from solid fats. Solid fats include butter, shortening, and lard.

Know what you eat. Your body will thank you.

SALT

Throughout history, people have been attracted to Team Salty. Salt was highly valued and even used as a form of money. It enhances the flavor of many foods. Sodium— a chemical found in salt—balances the fluids in your body. But people usually consume much more sodium than their bodies need. Too much sodium leads to heart disease, high blood pressure, and many other problems. Try not to add extra salt to foods, and keep an eye on food labels to check their levels of sodium.

55

TOOLS GLOSSARY

Baking pan
flat metal pan with high sides for baking cakes and brownies

Baking sheet
flat metal pan used to bake cookies and other baked goods

Blender
appliance with a rotating blade that mixes solids and liquids together

Colander
bowl dotted with holes to drain liquids from foods

Dry measuring cups
containers the size of specific standard measurements. Dry cups come in ¼ cup, ⅓ cup, ½ cup, and 1 cup sizes. Measure dry ingredients over an empty bowl, not over your mixture, in case of spills. Level off dry ingredients with a table knife.

Electric hand mixer
appliance that uses beaters to mix, blend, and whip foods

Hand blender
blender that you hold in one hand and insert into a bowl

Liquid measuring cup
container marked at intervals along the sides to accurately measure amounts of liquid. A liquid measuring cup is usually marked at ¼ cup, ⅓ cup, ½ cup, ⅔ cup, ¾ cup, and 1 cup intervals. Hold the cup at eye level to check the measurement.

Measuring spoons
spoons the size of specific standard measurements. Measuring spoons come in ¼ teaspoon, ½ teaspoon, 1 teaspoon, and 1 tablespoon measurements. There are 3 teaspoons in a tablespoon.

Microwave
appliance that cooks food with radio waves. Make sure the cup, bowl, or plate you use is microwave-safe. Microwaving heats food and the container it's in, so use oven mitts to remove it from the microwave.

Potato masher
tool used to crush soft foods into a lumpy mixture

Saucepan
round, deep metal pan with a handle
and a lid, used on a stovetop

Spatula
flat tool used to mix ingredients or
scrape the side of a bowl

Stockpot
round, deep metal pot used for making large
amounts of food, used on the stovetop

Turner
flat tool used to flip foods from one side
to the other or to remove foods from a pan

Vegetable peeler
tool that separates the peel or skin of
a fruit or vegetable from its flesh

Wire cooling rack
rack made of a grid of metal wires
that allows air to reach the top, bottom,
and sides of food to cool it quickly

TECHNIQUE GLOSSARY

Batter
mixture of dry ingredients and liquids that can be poured

Beat
stir very quickly to help add air to a mixture

Blend
mix together, often in a blender

Boil
heat until small bubbles form on the top of a liquid

Dice
cut into very small pieces

Dough
mixture that becomes stiff enough to form with your hands

Drain
remove liquid by pouring it off or placing it in a colander

Grate
cut into small thin strips. To grate foods, you rub them against a grater—a flat metal kitchen tool covered with tiny blades and holes.

Mash
squash a soft food into a lumpy mixture

Melt
heat a food to turn it from solid to liquid

Mince
cut into the finest, smallest pieces

Preheat
turn the oven on ahead of time so it reaches the correct temperature when you are ready to begin baking

Puree
blend a food until it is smooth

Slice
cut into thin pieces with a knife

Thaw
bring frozen food to room temperature

"To Taste"
to your liking. Recipes often leave the amount of seasoning ingredients up to the cook, so you can add more or less, depending on what you like.

READ MORE

Carle, Megan, and Jill Carle. *Teens Cook: How to Cook What You Want to Eat.* Berkeley, Calif.: Ten Speed Press, 2004.

Dunnington, Rose. *Big Snacks, Little Meals: After School, Dinnertime, Anytime.* New York: Lark Books, 2006.

Schwartz, Ellen. *I'm a Vegetarian: Amazing Facts and Ideas for Healthy Vegetarians.* Plattsburgh, N.Y.: Tundra Books, 2002.

Stern, Sam. *Real Food, Real Fast.* Cambridge, Mass.: Candlewick Press, 2008.

INTERNET SITES

Use FactHound to find Internet sites related to this book. All of the sites on FactHound have been researched by our staff.

Here's all you do:
Visit *www.facthound.com*
Type in this code: 9780756544065

ACKNOWLEDGEMENTS

Many thanks to friends and family members who sampled my creations and shared recipe advice. I am grateful to Paula Meachen, Patricia Rau, Denise Genest, and the Tuesday morning writers. Additional thanks to the teens of my neighborhood who e-mailed me lists of their favorite foods. An extra nod to Chris, Charlie, and Allison, who ate and drank the good and the bad and never held back their honest opinions.

Dana Meachen Rau

INDEX

Dana Meachen Rau

Dana Meachen Rau is the author of more than 250 books for children, from preschoolers to teens. She loves baking cookies, shopping at local farms, and growing tomatoes and basil in her backyard garden. Her favorite food by far is chocolate. Even in summer, she usually enjoys a steaming cup of hot cocoa every day.